Be The Moment

A Practical Guide To Being

Edward C. Leinartas

"Daddy'O"

DEDICATION

In appreciation for all those that have come before me, I give thanks for the structures and knowledge that has been explicated to date. It surely would prove more difficult if the sages, monks, and all the oral and written traditions were not in the overt consciousness of humanity. This inheritance has made my path easier as I hope that others may benefit from any catalyst that this text may provide.

Some notable influences that must be named are Sai Baba, Alan Watts, Eckhardt Tolle, Thich Nyat Kahn, and Pem Chodra. These beacons of light have guided me and millions of others in this search for Truth in the last 50 years.

It is interesting that this culture has been inculcating more of the term 'moment' in advertising and cultural media. This is no coincidence. The 100th monkey concept, where everyone is slowly figuring out that there is something there without necessarily talking to each other, is steadily achieving mass. This 'something' has a resonance and vitality that is not available anywhere else. It is the light coming in small but consistent doses that changes our awareness. As our culture grows, as our numbers increase, a critical mass is achieved where things just begin to happen and everyone 'gets it'. This effort is aimed at those upcoming moments. It is nonsectarian *and* interfaith in content. Any acceleration towards that goal helps everyone.

In my path I have had the opportunity to discuss this thinking (really non-thinking) for about the past 5 years on a consistent basis. My facilitation with others is with "the Energy" and distinctly not "my" energy. If it was "my" energy then we would not be here today. "The" energy is the Tao that cannot be named. It is there when I leave my ego out of the moment and allow "The" energy to Be. It is how it is. A successful contact with another also involves a moving aside of 'thinking you are right, absolutely' to an openness with reduced bias to new information. The blocking of Self is then removed from both parties allowing the 'flow' to abide. And it is always magnificent. The Energy speaks to the Energy. What I have to say is secondary and insignificant to what occurs at the energy level. Energy first, energy right, energy flowing, is what makes the words right and the actions solid.

This book is an attempt to extend the energy experience to more than the moments we feel after an experience of Being in the Moment. It is a set of questions to ask ourselves, to get out of our mind and out of a pattern of thinking/doing/experiencing into the Being/ non-thinking/experience. Without a strategy to get back to our Source, we may struggle for more unnecessary time figuring it out, if ever. This is based on my experience and I feel it is universal enough for others to find benefit as long as attachment is not too strong or defensive in the mind. Some people think that they have been hypnotized. I would agree they have been hypnotized by the mind and metaphors of unconscious doing. When you enter into the Presence you enter into a clear no mind (un-hypnotized) state.

It is advisable to process this book similar to how the classic "The Prophet" would be read. To speed read this text would assure the reader of *not* getting the message and intent. On the other hand, if we can 'be' with the ideas and challenge ourselves to test our assumptions, we will find benefit. Certainly, this book is not a 'classic'. However, contemplation of the ideas will give profit to the reader. Inculcate the contents, test everything out, and Be the Moment! 5-31-2012.

CONTENTS

ACKNOWLEDGMENTS

A special thanks for my wife Lynn is always appropriate due to the support system and platform to work having being provided to me on a daily basis. A kind thanks to Leela for saving the book and editing the errors out.

1 WHO ARE WE?

"Be yourself. Everyone else is already taken up." -
written on the temple walls 2010 Burning Man.

I am that. I am the I am. I am you and you are me.

Do we know who we really are? It is said that we are

three things: who we think we are, who others think we are, and who we really are. Who we think we are, is interesting because it is an 'idea' of who we are. It is mind-based and restricted to the context of the tool called the mind. It is a very limited, distorted, and a false sense of identity. Moreover, it is common and probably a part of our own definition of self. Who others think we are, is also limiting, projected, incomplete, biased, and a distorted picture of self. This definition can vary as widely as to whom you ask. It has little to no understanding of intention, reference and starting points, and is temporal even when it is comprehensive from multiple viewers.

Who we really are, is far more intriguing, assuming we are staying away from the two other attempts at clarification of self. First, there is a distinctive difference in that there is permanence to the structure, if we can use the dualistic term of structure.

Permanence is defined as timeless. To get a sense of timelessness, imagine that everyone alive today will no longer be alive in 120 years. Where do we get this idea that we shall live forever? We feel this, though there is no evidence for it whatsoever. It certainly can't be the body. And when we are in the body, we age, clearly revealing a depreciating outcome every time we look in the mirror. In so many ways we have a sense of self that really has not changed since as early as we can remember. We see the physical vehicle grow and change, get injured and recover, get education and socialization, and employment and roles in our life. But it really feels pretty much the same with the slight exceptions.

Why?

IF ENLIGHTENMENT IS NOT WHERE YOU ARE STANDING, WHERE WILL YOU LOOK?

Could it be we are so caught up with the grind of our daily life of quiet desperation that we never really take time to be with the most captivating part of our lives and existence here and now? We have excluded ourselves from nature creating a duality that is us against the environment. We believe we need to take from the environment to the degree that we exploit our own long-term good for very short-term purposes. We expose our weakness for unbridled greed. Those new pair of shoes looks real good! It goes past the environment to the exploitation of people, even our own family. This dualistic separate sense of being and self is the problem. This dualism conveniently hides our discontent and malice to self and others. This normality is conveniently commonplace allowing further inappropriate indulging in the compromised sense of self. Is this the best we can do? This is truly who we think we are in our lives?! We are dead to our real selves and dead to the connectivity of all of us to all of us.

We truly are none of the above. Deep beneath the superficiality of this drama is who we really are in this moment, this presence, this awareness, this plenum of bliss. We are beyond the petty limitations of these temporary phenomena. However, we don't know what we don't know. Or really we don't know what we did once know but have forgotten. In fact, once you open up and really listen with less mind, you will remember again. You will begin to score this feeling that feels so right and is so integrated and is so you. You will know (without the mind telling you).

Shivaratri is an annual Hindu festival that celebrates the advantage of the moon being most distant from the earth. This optimal seasonal distance is believed to help us grow spiritually in those moments due to the moon's influence on the mind being the least. This allows more opportunity to see things in an unfettered way and to accelerate spiritual progress. There may be argument as to the significance of this thinking but where this idea has merit is the direct influence of the mind on our lives. The point being that we need to decrease the influence of the mind on our self so we can better realize our Being. When we push the mind, the mind pushes back, hard! The mind is

energy. Energy does not like to get pushed. Energy likes to be led. Why are we pushing? We cannot defeat the mind with the mind. We cannot find ourselves when we use the limitation called the mind. The mind is a sophisticated tool like a CMOS (Complementary Metal Oxide Semiconductor). The CMOS is an image sensor that converts light into electronic bits of information to allow digital single lens reflex cameras phenomenal picture quality. This image sensor can convert reality into beautiful selective shots that are very accurate. The mind, as well, is quite good at memorizing events, patterns, and exceptions as well as employing reason and discrimination. These devices, the CMOS sensor and the mind are tools we should use. The tools should <u>not</u> use us. These tools are here to serve us. When we are through taking pictures we need to set the camera down. If we continue to carry around the camera to the washroom, or washing the car, or painting the fence, it becomes awkward. However, we do the analog precisely with the mind. We never turn it off. It rules us. We use it to process everything no matter how inappropriate the process. Our society believes that we must always think. How ridiculous?! What happens when we stop thinking? (Do we know how?) We won't die. To answer the question, we have consciousness that allows the mind to operate. We do not need the mind to have consciousness. So when we temporarily let the mind go we experience the depth of silence and Presence of our Being, we set the tool down, so to speak. We do not lose the ability to pick up the tool when we need it next. By doing this we use the tool appropriately. The trick comes in on knowing how to set the tool down. Picking it up we know too well.

The process of engaging consciousness and disengaging the mind, are the most problematic of tasks to learn. In order to begin to dislodge erroneous conclusions about how things work, especially in relation to the mind and ego, we must look at the conditions we set for optimization of either the Being state or the mind state. These conditions are broken down for sake of understanding. These conditions are not as discrete in reality as delineated here. In order to get a deeper understanding of the fact that we ARE NOT the mind and do not need the continued unabated disruption that the mind causes, we will separate things out for clarity.

Earlier we indicated how strong of an influence the mind is on our spiritual progress. One of the biggest things to get right is the understanding of time zones.

First question, are we in the right time zone right now? There are three basic time zones, two of which are unrealities. As much as the past and future are unrealities, we abide in them constantly. Let's look at percentages. How much time do you spend in the past and how much time do you spend in the future? Roughly, I would suggest we spend about 45% in the past and 45% in the future with the remaining 10% fleetingly going in and out of the Present. The two unrealities capture most of our commitments and life.

These are not real nor are they a viable place to be. They are the hallmark of the mind and ego's unfettered zones of activity. These specious time zones are unreal because they do not really exist. *It's what we think, not what is.*

In a recent conversation I had at Whole Foods with an employee, I was told about a situation that was described as unfair due to a presumed inability to go to a training that would enhance the employee's self-worth. Initially the manager stated that training was possible. Later, after finding out the training was similar to a past training, the manager appeared to be declining the request. The employee told me how she was rehearsing the statements she would deliver upon contact with the manager. Nothing was certain except uncertainty. I suggested it would be presumptuous to come in loaded versus completely open. Too much thinking and way too little 'being' was in the offing. This is a situation where we overvalue thinking and undervalue 'being'. Being is in tune with what is and therefore always more relevant in the moment. The employee was receptive to the restructuring. We need to be receptive to not concluding or assuming how others will think or do, especially if we want to connect. Subsequently, the employee related a chain of events that underscored the brilliance of being and oneness of the universe.

The third time zone, of course, is the Present. The eternal now is always infinitely ours. It is ours in the sense of everything, not in the sense of ownership. Being in the right time zone assures us of being an integrated personality with a constancy of being informed by the power of nature itself. It is the connection to whom we are, always. Be that.

2 **Patterns of Behavior** –"What has been showing up for me as a pattern and what am I doing about it?"

ı **In order to more fully understand consciousness, we have to look at the reality of how we are unconscious. When we go through life, we learn to adapt and short-cut common basic premises of doing things. That is, different things we have to do a lot of and things we first have to understand, before continued movement and growth. George Lakoff, neuro-linguist at U of C Berkeley, works in the field where the intersection of neurosciences and language sciences come together. He** suggests that we may form a basic neural path for processing specific brain activities. This is especially true if we continue to repeat the brain activity, the path becomes an established circuit. This circuit kicks in subsequent specific tasks with an increased efficiency in brain activity. Developmentally around ten years of age we move from concrete thinking to abstract thinking. We begin to reason through the use of metaphors, inductive and deductive reasoning. But it is the metaphors that take us out of the robotic into the conceptual. Love, morality and dharma are made possible through this system. This system gives us an expanded understanding while potentially limiting our consciousness through the efficiency of adaptation.

How we operate, is affected with an efficiency that eventually eliminates the question of why. We do not know 'why' we are thinking this conclusion anymore because we have done it so often it is automatic. We lose consciousness because it is sublimated to adaptation and metaphor. And that maybe is OK, as if in driving, and it may not be OK as in driving (or other activity where we need to be present). Too much adaptation can easily result in a loss of awareness and dependence on routine, patterns and / or brain circuits. We may believe in an idea but we have always believed in this idea since it was given to us from our parents. In certain instances, we really no longer can logically justify it relative to some of our other thinking. The big deal is that we are not even aware of the conflicts between ideas. As a matter of fact, George Lakoff suggests we are more than 95% unconscious.

Most people believe advertising works on influencing the population to purchase products or

services. However, some

people do not believe it works on them. Ask them what

kind of cell phone they have or want, what brand of

vodka/coffee they drink, what their favorite TV show

is? To think that we do not have unconscious desires,

thoughts, and patterns, is to not really know ourselves

very well. It is important to first understand and

accept that *we don't know what we are not aware of in*

our own life. Once we 'get' that we don't know, then we

can begin to know. Awareness is the tool we will be

accessing all the time to increase our consciousness.   It

is important to know that we probably do not have as

much consciousness as we think we do. When someone

says that we do not have the awareness we think we do,

we probably process that through the mind and ego and have a reaction like, "No, not me man." This is typical. The reality is what neurolinguistics indicates. We are over 95% unconsciousness. Generally, it is my conclusion, that unless we have been practicing constant integrated awareness every moment, we have been missing a whole lot.

UNCERTAINTY –Why do we want to abandon the Moment?

The resistance to uncertainty is interesting. Do we ever not do it, that is, stop resisting? What is it we are resisting? Is it uncertainty? Why do we need to have certainty? Do we need certainty to maintain equilibrium? Will equilibrium break down if we have too much uncertainty? But what if we had too much certainty? What would happen to our lives given we had all the predictability we could ever have? Would we find life interesting? Would we just quit because we knew what would be next every time? Would we find life challenging anymore? How long could you go on like this in a predictable world? There would be no more resistance because there would be nothing to resist due to no options except what is laid out. Could you stand it for more than a week? I think not. But then why do we resist the basic mechanism of the universe –uncertainty? Is it the basic mechanism of the universe?

The universe, the world we live in and its associated patterns and laws, is forever changing. Expansion and change are constants that science and to a certain degree religion, have articulated for millennia. Buddhists iterate the permanence of change. Expansion could be said to be a part of change. Change is one thing I think everyone really does agree upon. The other assumption here is the predictability of change. Can anyone really predict the future reliably all the time? The record speaks for itself. We can predict some general patterns but we can't even predict weather reliably. We can predict some cause and effect to a limited extent but to predict the next 5 minutes proves difficult in too many scenarios.

So here we are, wanting to know what will happen next so we can better regulate our lives day-to-day. We want to know if our kids can afford to go to college, if we will be able to retire, and if Social Security will be here in 25 years.

However, if everything was laid out as described above, we could not live under those circumstances. Why? Uncertainty, in relationship to change, is permanent. We constantly resist uncertainty and thereby resist the weight of the entire universe. If we think it through, we would not want to have the Stepford Wife model of existence. Where would the challenge be? And we resist the Moment looking for something else in the future. We are not Present because we choose to leave, *thinking* we are dissatisfied. Uncertainty is the element in the game called life that must be there in order for it to work and be in conformance with the integrity of the whole universe. Without 'uncertainty' we would stop playing the game, period.

Think of when you play chess, or checkers, or a card game and the inevitable is there before the game is actually over. What happens? There is a concession and the game is over before it's all played out. When the future is so predictable, we quit. Life is not worth living.

We need 'uncertainty'. We need to totally accept 'uncertainty' as a legitimate game element. When we do that, we stop resisting the whole universe and our life is not so much a struggle than a flow. We understand that we can play the game better when we fully accept the rules. Better still, love the 'uncertainty'! Then there is no resistance. We are then Acting, acting like the universe, not reacting against the universe. We act as if we understand the game and leave failed strategies for lesser players who do not understand.

So, when the drama hits us on the stage of life, we are either in the game or not (that is, resisting the uncertainty). If we are truly in the Moment, we will engage fully with uncertainty like an accomplished actor, enjoying the challenge and using the knowledge of the game to advantage. There would be no worrying. There is only Being. When there is Being, the Moment is full, we are fully aware, having the time of our lives (bliss). What beauty there is in life when you don't worry about the future! To suggest that one is worrying in the Present is to be deluded by the mind. When everything is satisfied in 'the' state of consciousness there cannot be such a thing as fretting.

When we embrace the Presence, we concurrently begin to love the uncertainty. In Aikido it is said that the safest spot is under the killing blade. Be that bold and beautiful energy.

Play the game. If we go to a play in a theatre, we understand that we will begin to suspend our belief upon the commencement of the play. We all agree. That's the game. If the actors are superb, believable, and doing their best impersonations of their assigned character, then we applaud them and thank them for giving us a good evening. We like that we bought what they were selling us, in terms of reality. It was entertaining and now the play is over we return to our real lives. Our lives are very much like the actors on a stage taking their cues from some director that you do not see onstage. We are playing roles in the drama of our so-called lives and we believe the roles to be real.

What do I mean? They aren't real?! Just *imagine*

your life *is* a role on the stage and it's your job to play

it as brilliantly as possible. The Director is The Energy

or The Being state. It is you in your permanence. The

temporary phenomenon of your life is your life. We

'act' brilliantly when we feed the actor with the

Director's guidance. Without this guide you will be a

poor performer because you have no direction. The

connection between you (the actor) and The Director is

essential to success. Let's throw a twist in here. If you

went to the Lyric Opera in Chicago and watched a

performance of "The Marriage of Figaro", the set

would be mesmerizing, the actors dressed to era

standards. The singing/acting would be world class. And then one of the actors in a difficult scene commits suicide. What? It was real! Oh, that wasn't in the script?! Why did the actor ruin the opera/play for everyone? The show had to stop.

We must not forget that this is just a play, but at the same time, we be convincing and play the game. The role may be difficult but that role is not who we are at the deepest level. We do not and should not forget who we are, all the time. Again, with an inviolable connection to the Director, we would never do anything contrary to the Director, because we are the Director and not the role. To destroy an innocent body is a misplaced understanding of reality/role and the vagaries of temporary phenomena. Love the uncertainty. It is acceptance of the cosmic play and there for the evolution of our Spirit.

3 The vectors of energy. "What am I sourcing?"

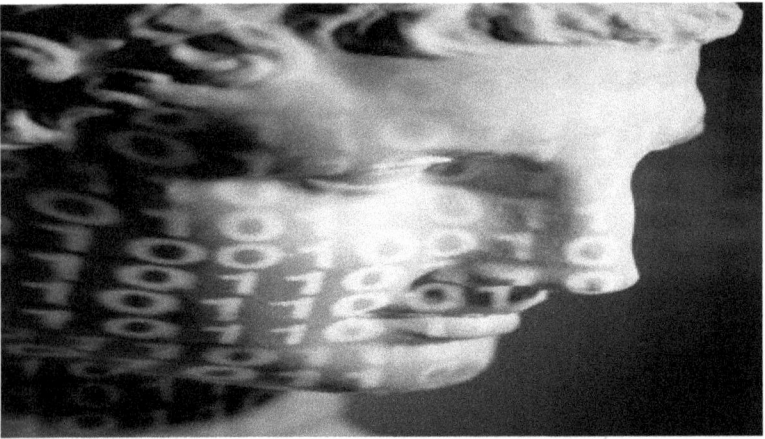

re. l

What am I sourcing, means to ask what is informing me every moment? What energy is giving us our direction? This is the cold truth for self. What really is feeding us in the Moment is the question. What is filling and thrilling our hearts? Or, possibly more accurately, what is feeding us in our unreality of self? The 'unreality' of self, because we are abiding in the unrealities of past and present, most of the time. We are probably in the Moment only for a fleeting moment, not as an ongoing state of consciousness. So, if we are probably not in the Moment most of the time, we have to be feeding our Self something that is a diminished substitute for Being. Perhaps, quiet desperation, finding self in the desire of a good future, feeling needy, or just accepting the underlying misery of existence, is what informs us, more or less, constantly.

What is sourcing us or what could be sourcing us constantly, is cathecting (charging with a specific vibration) of energy that has profound implications. If we look at the moments that pass, and that fact that every moment is a creative moment where we are cathecting and endowing it with a specific vibration, we are then creating constantly. This creation becomes our life, our script to follow. When we corrupt our creation with energy that is sourced from compromised conditions, we engender further corruption for our destiny. If we are constantly finding self in the future by saying to ourselves, when I get this car (house, clothes, camera, 3D tv, education, job, etcetera) I'll get what I really need and be happy. And the beat goes on. No enduring happiness arrives and we are back at the desiring of finding that something external that will fill in this missing part. It won't happen. It can't happen.

Fact is, it has already happened or more accurately, Is
happening Now. If it's happening now, why can't we
get it, we ask. Yes, it is happening Now. And right now
we are directly in the way of fully experiencing It. We
need to get out of the way.

A friend and I went to do a test drive of several
high end cars at an event that was monitored by
experienced race drivers.

There was a road course and an opportunity to indulge

in throttling these vehicles while receiving expert feedback from the veteran drivers. One piece of advice that was given me was to let the vehicle's engineering do most of the driving and when necessary, make the turn, push the accelerator, but for the most part let the car drive itself. If I did too much, I would overwhelm the engineering built into the car and the car would be ineffective on the road course, resulting in a slower time. I needed to get out of the way most of the time. Life is engineered to work effortlessly for us. The facts are that we do not have to regulate our body's temperature, growth, healing, and etcetera. We need to let life take care of the 'how', the part that our interference would undermine. We are not capable of matching the power, grace, and timing of the universe. It is the job of the universe to handle the enormous complexity of 'how' it all goes down.

In life our greatest enemy is our self. In martial arts, it is said, to kill the enemy within, we will have achieved victory. There is no greater enemy. If every morning when we get up, we have resistance to do our meditation, Yoga, and mile run, and then we cut through it all with forward mind; we will then establish the pattern for vision and getting beyond obstacles that will invariably be there. Over time, the obstacles become insignificant. The greatest obstacle, ego, will be removed when we see it is seen as an obstacle that is resisting the drama. The drama is going to happen according to the Director. Get the ego out of the way and listen to the Director. All this happens on the inside with the outside giving us some clues. The confusion is usually, first, the confusion over whom we are when we try to see who we are. Second, when we try to see what is fueling us now and cannot accurately conclude where the energy is coming from. These are the questions of life. We are going from Self to Self. Get out of the way. We are not this mind-created archetype called the ego. We are not mind-based. *I am That,* is who we are always. Our source is the omnipotence of life itself. It is the same energy that shines the sun, that moves the earth, and that provides the receptors in the liver for LDL cholesterol, all without any apparent effort on our part. Be that. Be that source because you are that source. Know thyself, first.

There is current thinking in the psychology field of substituting good thoughts for bad thoughts. This may work to a certain degree because the mind is capable of only thinking one thought at a time. It is certainly a worthwhile venture if you can overcome the negative patterns of thinking and behavior that this

34

daily grind of existence has wrought to date.

Additionally, we have the burden of being able to see clearly enough to make the substitution when necessary. This certainly is a better option than doing nothing. When we are substituting thoughts, one for another, we are still in the content and context of the mind. The mind is an endpoint.

The mind also probably has become the starting point due to not having a connection with the depth of Being. In the case of the starting point and the endpoint both co-occurring in the mind, we struggle with the tool called the mind disregarding the connection and energy that is already integrated. This is 'doing' energy with no reference to 'Being' energy. The solution lies not in going to the endpoint for remediation, but <u>going to the true starting point and reestablishing that connection.</u>

Be the 'Be' and then do the 'do'. We cannot do the 'Be'.

We can do the 'do' and never really get informed by the 'Be'. So, to fix the endpoint is weak, especially when it is uninformed by Presence. When we team-up with the presence of the Moment, we can be constantly informed by the Being state achieving an effortless and natural integration of Self that does so without coercing a tool, like the mind. Why change the qualities of the tool when you can opt for streaming consciousness that is complete and a precursor to the mind? To argue for changing the qualities of the tool is to argue for saying that we are the mind, when in fact, it is the lie we have believed unconditionally for all of our lives. We must stop being controlled by the mind. When we are not controlled by the mind, then we can use the tool as our consciousness, our higher self, requires. See what is being sourced. Make the choice, to get the Awareness of the Moment and stream and load-up the real you.

There is an assumption about the universe that needs mentioning. We probably think that events are unrelated, that they are discrete, and that there is no continuity except man-made continuity. Worse, we believe in coincidences, not the underlying unity in the diversity.

Contrarily, even modern physics applauds the unity in the diversity. The Unified Field Theory, the simplest and most complete theory, unites General Relativity with Quantum mechanics. This is big in academia due to scientists looking for the underlying connections in four dimensions. Cause and effect are calculable. In our everyday lives we create, sustain, and attract people, situations, and karma. The sustenance of our lives is connected to the unseen, profound, and omnipresence of greater Self. To presume that it is happenstance and totally random is to deny the Intelligence that is subtle and not obvious, that is both unformed and formed, and that is as synchronous, mathematically elegant, and geometrically beautiful as possible. Look in our past for and see the extraordinary circumstances that have already occurred in our life. See in the Present, what is always miraculous timing in our lives right now. It is always there. We must be in the reality of the Moment to better see the less than obvious but constant underscoring of unity that the universe provides us. This occurs on a moment-by- moment basis. Remove the ego (without pushing), see the Self (through Awareness), Be in the Moment (the right time zone), sustain a constant fueling from Self, and watch the miraculous movement of the universe in our lives.

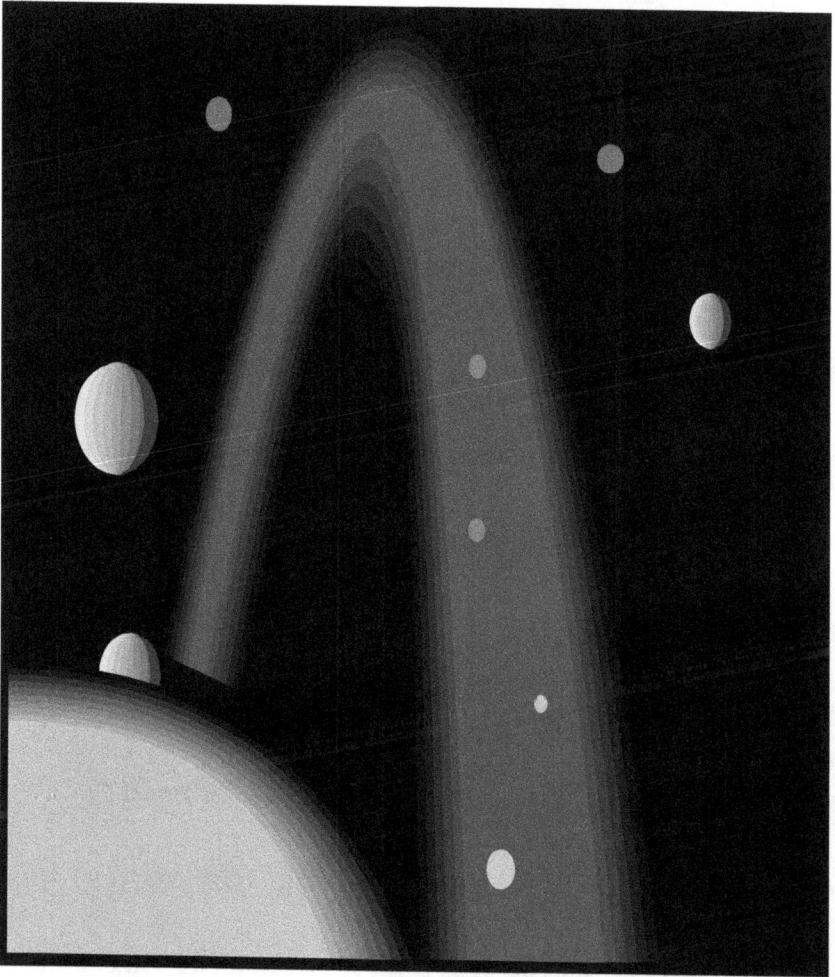

4 TOOLS FOR THE JOURNEY. "WHAT MODALITIES AM I USING?"

WHEN THE ONLY TOOL YOU HAVE IS A HAMMER, THEN EVERYTHING STARTS TO LOOK LIKE A HIPPIE." UNKNOWN AUTHOR A LA BURNING MAN.

I Satchitananda is a sacred word because it is pointing to the moon or higher Self. Of course the word is only a word and should not be worshipped per se. It is of East Indian origin, that is, the word is of East Indian origin. The experience, the moon, is indigenous to the human race, it Is. The experience does not need the word. There is no need to argue about this word or any other. As sacred as the word is, it is only the finger pointing to the moon. Be the Moon. Be the Be.

The word Satchitananda is one word with three (3) components. It is one word with three components due to three (3) things or processes going on at the same time. If one process is there, and if it is valid, then the other two (2) processes will be there. They all co-occur together. In terms of discussion and elucidation, we take these apart. In practice, all three (3) processes are always present. Again, if any one of the three is not present then there is no validity to this experience meeting the full criteria of the experience of Satchitananda. Know this when we traverse looking at each piece.

"Sat" refers to the Being state of consciousness.

"Chit" refers to the component process otherwise called Awareness. "Ananda" refers to the part of consciousness labeled as Divine Unalloyed Bliss. So when we are in the Being state, when we are the element process called Awareness, and when we are experiencing the overwhelming bliss of Self, then we are having the consciousness of Satchitananda. It is sometimes referred as an 'altered' state of consciousness. This type of reference serves to make this state of being as unapproachable by mere mortals. This is a disservice. This consciousness is as basic and seminal as it gets. It is who you are, more than anything else, than what you may 'think' you are now.

This is a super natural state that we as humans have had and lost for millennia. This 'lost' state was never really gone but hidden and depreciated by the ego and distortion of the unrealities of the past/future. It is as permanent as it gets. It is a source bigger than the actual universe seen and unseen. It Is. Religions are based on It but not defined by religions, although attempts are always made.

Awareness or "Chit" is probably not the awareness you 'think' it is. If you think awareness, then you are "thinking awareness" and attempting to enslave awareness into a framework that is finite and mind-based. When we do this we automatically limit the infinite to the weakness of a framework that cannot begin to give us the clarity of Being we need. It, in this case, is an awareness that is insufficient for seeing and making efficacious changes in our lives. And primarily the change we are looking for is one that will satisfy us in a profound way that nothing external can ever do for us, period.

So the 'thinking' error goes something like this or a similar variant. I want to be more aware. (This is the 'nice' desire we have that is mind-based.) So we are feeling 'needy' and unfulfilled. We beckon our traditional mind-based resources and say to self, I will begin practicing the techniques I just read in the library, and begin having increased awareness that is essential for my growth. We garner our desire and will and firmly begin to become more aware. In this scenario, where are we using our so-called awareness? We are still in the mind. We are working with the mind exclusive of our Beingness. This is a little more like self-observation. The process of seeking is reduced by the nature of the tool, i.e. the mind. The mind has great utility but not here. Here it is an absolute

impediment if not properly handled. Awareness to the

mind is a threat to its dominance and control. The

mind will never allow the compromised type of

awareness to defeat its parameters. And it will invoke

its parameters both gross and subtle. Awareness is

severely limited in its breadth and will never be enough

to overcome the mind while residing in the mind. That

is the problem.   So when we use Awareness, we don't *use*

Awareness, because Awareness cannot be *used* in the sense

of what It Is. We <u>can</u> use awareness with the mind. But it

is *not* the Awareness we are looking for! The Awareness we

are looking for is part of the Being/Awareness/Bliss trifecta

of being Self. It is accessed through the Being state of 'no

mind'. Satchitananda does not need mind to exist. Mind

does need Sathchitananda to exist. So Satchitananda is the

preexisting condition of Self and mind. Again mind is just a tool. "I want awareness!" Get rid of the 'I'. Get rid of the 'want'. Yes, then there Is the Awareness. The problems come in terms of using the wrong processes to which we are inured and conditioned to the point of radical unconsciousness. Awareness is as effortless as your signature. You don't have to think about it. You just do it effortlessly. It is effortless because it is you. When we are using the mind to find awareness, then it is analogous to us signing someone else's signature. Effortlessness is way gone. We are trying and doing. We are not Being and effortlessly doing. 'Being' always comes first. It has to, due to having the imperative connection to Self. Without this connection we are sincerely impaired. When we are properly connected to Self, we are then able to proceed with 'doing'. The 'Being' never stops. The Awareness of Being is just as constant. Can Awareness be done from 9 to 5? It can but it wouldn't make any sense to do it that way. When you understand (not so much in the 'mind') that you are employing the correct process, it would be ridiculous to do otherwise. When you have discovered the S.O.S. (Superior Operating System), why would a much more primitive system continue to be appealing? The Awareness, the Being, and the Bliss inform us through consciousness of Self and ego. We can see the mind, the thoughts, and the ego without being any of that due to the lack of attachment/identification with these archetypes, all temporary in nature. The act of identification itself is a commitment away from the Being. "Being" does not need identification. It just is. When you are aligned with the entire universe, and then some, why would you go against all that, even for a short period of time? You are all 'that'.

MEDITATION –CONTEMPLATIVE ARTS

Here the idea of a finger pointing to the moon would label the finger as the technique and the moon as what really must be focused upon. Contemplative arts, summarily known as meditation, are as vast as saying "sports" and assuming that everyone knows what specific activity one is talking about. There are many techniques and variations on contemplative options. Whirling dervishes (Sufism), Namasmarayana (Hinduism), Sweat Lodge (American Indian), Trance (African Shamanism), Voodou (Haiti), Chanting (Nichiren Buddhism), and others are fingers pointing to the moon. Many techniques, mentioned and unmentioned can take one to the moon. One technique is not necessarily better than the other. At one level it is all technique, technique mattering less than process. This is the place where a categorical error often takes place. We go and sit straight, spine straight, relaxed. We get comfortable. First we get our body out of the way. We connect our tongue to the top of our mouth, completing the meridian circuit of governing vessel to conception vessel. This fusion of meridians creates a balance between the Yin and Yang energies of the body. Our breath slows naturally. Slowing the breath further relaxes the body and begins to slow the mind. Once the body is out of the way then the mind is next. Especially in the beginning, the mind needs an object in which to focus on. It can be the breath, a mantra, a chant, a candle flame, a mandala, or a very specific methodology like Vipasasana meditation. Once the mind is engaged, then a period of time like 20 minutes is recommended to dive into the depth of silence. Once here, this is where the categorical error is made. We are doing meditation with all the procedures of a bureaucrat. Meditation cannot take place under these circumstances. A different process is necessary for success and it is not 'doing'. One cannot 'do' meditation. One must 'be' meditation. It is no longer a set of steps. It Is.

Why meditate? This is an important question. What we are getting at when we use contemplative arts is the deep silence within that is the force that underlies everything in the universe, seen and unseen. It is the 'is', it is the I am. When we are busy living our lives of quiet desperation, we are too busy doing and finding Self in the past and the future unrealities. The time dedicated to some intensive 'Being' is important. Transcendental Meditation had an analogy of a handkerchief being dipped into an inkwell and absorbing the ink through the fibers of the cloth. Not unlike taking a dip in the Self. Using the infrastructure of meditation we break down tedious vasanas and control of the mind over our Being and our Being state of consciousness. At a very advanced level, we do not need the infrastructure anymore because we have become the Light (You see the Light, the Light is in you, and then you are the Light.). Meditation then, is constant in the tasks of everyday life. The building is erected and stable and the scaffolding is no longer necessary. Liberation from the chains of ego-based consciousness is achieved.

EXAMPLES OF TECHNIQUE

Sitting and counting your breaths, repeating a word in your mind continuously, and going through the chakras with sound and vision —are three techniques that anyone can use. No one technique is necessarily better than another. The best technique is the one that works effectively for you. If you manifest a revolution in your heart then you have the right technique, mantra, or whatever is getting the mind and little self out of the way. There are many paths up the mountain but there is only one mountain.

The technique with probably the least embellishment

and least doctrine is just sitting and counting your breaths. Sit comfortably with your spine straight and body relaxed. This comfort can take place in a chair or on a cushion (zabuton) on the floor. Eyes may be closed or slightly closed, but relaxed. Breathing can be either with the mouth open or closed, whichever is comfortable. Slow, deep breaths with distinct inhalations and exhalations, are rendered. Begin with purging (exhaling) the breath, then count 1 inhalation, then 1 exhalation, then 2 inhalation, 2 exhalation until reaching 10 exhalation. Upon reaching the 10th exhalation, the next count is 1 inhalation, 1 exhalation, again, until reaching 10 exhalation, and so on. Initially what will happen is we will forget to go to 1 and instead go to 11. . . Gently go to 1 inhalation when you figure out your error. During this process there is just sitting. There is no 'doing' except for sitting. Stop 'doing' except for sitting.

The next technique is the recitation of a mantra (a sound that is pleasing to you and perhaps has some spiritual significance). Mantras were traditionally selected for the student by a guru relative to the temperament of the student. Some mantras were selected based on astrology. The point being is that you are going to be inculcating this sound continuously for a period of 20 to 40 minutes per day for as many as 40 years. Therefore it is sensible that the sound and meaning be selected with forethought. After adjusting the body to a comfort level that does not promote sleep, and choosing a time that is not right after a large meal, sit straight with the spine in the body's plumb line. Eyes should be closed, especially in the beginning. Without subvocalizing or lip-syncing, repeat the mantra continuously inside your mind. If you drift off in thought or run into 'no thought', gently bring the recitation back once your awareness is regained. The mantra becomes the object of the meditation allowing the mind to become preoccupied with it. This engagement of the mind is necessary to experience the consciousness surrounding the

mind. The ability to leave

the mind, with its contents often playing *a horror movie

inside*, is now enabled. You do not need to change the

movie so much as to leave the theater. The right use of the

mind is inevitable upon using the appropriate connection.

Enjoy the show. Om sweet om.

The 3rd technique is using the specific center of our chakras (Wheels) to focus mind upon. Below the chakras and their correlate significance are defined. This is similar to the scale in Western Thought; Maslow's hierarchy of needs. Abraham Maslow began with physiological

Figure 1   *LA VA RA YA HA HUM*

demands working up to self-actualization. Similarly, ancient practices began with the following. The 1st chakra is survival; 2nd is procreation/sex; 3rd is power; 4th is love; 5th is communication; 6th is spirituality; and 7th is higher consciousness. In the subtle body, it is theorized that we have seven major chakras starting from the base of the spine, through the torso, to the top of the head (Crown Chakra). The meditation involves going through 6 chakras, visualizing the exact location of each one to the body while saying the ancient sound associated with each particular chakra. The base of the spine (the perineum) has the sound "la", the area 2 inches below the navel (prostrate/ovaries) is sounded with "va", the navel area (liver, pancreas, spleen, kidneys, adrenal, suprarenal) is pronounced "ra", the heart region is chanted "ya", the throat region (thyroid) is said as "ha" and the last sound is "hum" which is either correlated with the 6th chakra in between the eyebrows (pineal, pituitary), or correlated with the top of the skull at the 7th chakra as "om". The choice of going with either the 6th or 7th chakra is presumably best decided astrologically. The meditation begins with eyes closed with the basic settling of the body. The mind is directed to locate internally the body geography while commencing with the particular sound. The movement begins at the lower chakra with finishing at the 6th or 7th chakra. Then going

back down from the top chakra back to the lowest chakra

and resuming that sequence like a ladder, up and down.

With the last technique especially, but really all

techniques for gathering the mind, there is a story that

illustrates what is going on and underscores the previous

points made. There was a king in a faraway land a long,

long time ago. His kingdom was vast and he needed some

help with his infrastructure. The sidewalks were crumbling, the bridges were unsafe, the buildings had graffiti, and there was a lot of deferred maintenance that need to be addressed expeditiously. So much so that the king knew he needed some divine intervention to fix this hot mess. Ego in hand and prostrations and petitions to follow, the king was granted an audience with the One. The One had heard the request and informed the humbled king that he can have help in the form of a tireless worker that WILL get everything straight. The king had his doubts, but said OK. He will take this worker despite thinking that this worker was incapable of finishing even half the tasks that were in front of him. The One cautioned the king. Do not be misled by the frail, nondescript personage in front of you, this servant shall meet the tasks at hand. And in so doing he will kill you if you do not give him enough work. The king was overconfident in his estimate of work and worker, and off he went, thanking the One. The servant immediately went to work kung-fuing and tearing up the tasks at hand. He was so agile that he scared the king into *now* believing that he would fulfill all that was in front of him. Hurriedly, the king went back to see the One and begged forgiveness for not believing what the One had forecast. The One accepted the apology and commenced a solution for the king. The king was directed to build a ladder going up 9 feet and a ladder going down 9 feet. When the servant was complete in his duties he would be directed to climb up the ladder and when he reached the top, he would be required to go down the ladder. This would go on and on until the servant was ready to resume working on productive tasks.

The moral of this story is to not let the mind recreate and control us when it is idle. The technique for controlling the mind is to give the mind an object on which to concentrate, thereby using the mind appropriately with no harm to us. Remember: it is just a tool. It is not 'us'.

5 –Practice Makes Perfect. "What is showing up?

In my job as a supervisor, I ended up with problems that needed a more creative solution. Often this takes the form of people loaded with negative energy that would be obvious to any observer. This negative loading, in my rendering, is valuable because it is glaring and easily quantified. The problem is not hidden and is loudly articulated in no uncertain terms. How beautiful! I always wanted to thank these people for making my job easier. I did not usually have to encourage the articulation. One event has the front desk calling me and needing my services because of a complaint about an officer. The gentleman wanted to speak to a supervisor because the officer was not giving satisfactory resolution. There was some disruption in the waiting area relative to this individual. The probationer approached me rising from his seat, and laying on the complaint. I stood there calm, listening, and silent while he ranted his frustration about waiting 3 hours every time he came in. He went on uninterrupted for about 45 seconds with the waiting area watching the scene. H e then stopped, waited a couple of more seconds, and then stated to me "Aren't you going to say anything, or are you going to stand there?" I immediately rejoined, calmly, "You were talking at me, not with me." Continuing, "If you want to talk with me, I'll talk with you." Now I did not think of anything when he was ranting. I was watching myself watching myself as he was complaining. What I said was spontaneous and unrehearsed. And it came out with the strength of Truth because it was true. I had no plan coming in on how to handle this complaint. Awareness of 'me' was far more important in this success than going outside the

Moment to find a solution. The rejoinder just popped from my lips. The situation progressed positively from that point on with the officer returning at the optimum time and engaging the probationer with success, exchanging good energy and producing a sufficient report.

What is showing up is the beauty of the Moment. There appears to be a risk at not reacting soon enough to sound competent. The reaction is what we do constantly. The reaction is what we don't even know we do. We act with reaction to the point that there is no action. When we engage in Awareness it is easier to see if we are connected to Self. If we are disconnected we can reconnect, especially if we know the way. Awareness is the Moment. Awareness is the secret of the Moment. In most cases we react, rather immediately, and unconsciously. What is showing up most of the time is what we practice most of the time, e.g. reaction. Have you watched yourself enough to really see that it is reaction 90% of the time? The tool of Awareness can hasten the demise of reaction as in the above example and in the one that follows. Action is what is usually more powerful than reaction. Being is action.

There was a call from a State's Attorney from another county inquiring about the ownership of an intrastate probation case. The information was accessible and given to the inquirer. While processing this information we engaged in discussion about energy, particularly energy indigenous to us as individuals. The attorney posited a question. If your energy is so-so and the judge's energy is not good, how would you handle the situation given some need to problem-solve? Plugging in

Awareness of Self at that moment, I felt that the issue is usually more resolvable if we start with ourselves and see our own characterizations of energy more clearly in the situation stated. The attorney needed to see and focus on self, more than she was focusing on the recalcitrant judge. If we focus our awareness on self, we see our reaction we are having with the judge. We see our reaction flow through us. There is no denial and there is no acting out. It all occurs on the inside and no one but us sees all this business. However, we, by seeing more clearly, are not reacting the old fashioned way we normally would without awareness. We change the dynamic of the relationship immediately and in a profound way. The energy that is exchanged is palpably different and more aware. We have defeated what we should always defeat, unconsciousness and reactivity.

Effortlessness and trust in the universe goes hand-in-hand in dealing with life's everyday situations. A few years before my father had transitioned; I had the privilege of working with him to get him proper medical treatment, confront hoarding, clean and sell his houses, follow-up on his care, and finalize his estate. This was a labor-intensive work that spanned a period of 5 continuous years. My travel to Florida to work the solutions had ranged from 1 time per month to 3 times per month with time stretching from a couple of days to a couple of weeks. For some of this time I had utilized the same cab driver consistently for trips to and from the airport. When arriving in the Tampa area I came with seemingly insurmountable problems and goals that needed to be achieved, that had no obvious solution. How was I going to get my father to get care for his obsessive hoarding? How will I get him to take any medication that would be prescribed to him? How will I clean his house if he fights me doing it? Where will I throw out his accumulation of roomfuls of garbage? How will the city work with me or against me in remedying these housing violations? How will I pay for things that are delinquent without his help? How will I get his cooperation to do anything? A lot of 'how' questions always hanging out. The issues and complexities did not relent until it was all over. The cab driver heard my issues coming in and the difficulties in achieving them, basically the 'how's'. On the return trip I would relate the solutions that had been achieved. And there were solutions, each time.

What I did was first determine what had to be accomplished each trip. Certain goals had to be achieved each trip. These tasks and specifics were outcome based. I did not have the details to as to 'how' they would be achieved. This not knowing the 'how' was the methodology for every trip but one. Not knowing was often not deliberate. Often I just had no clue. Over time I realized that it was useful to come in this way. Remarkably the impossible was getting done each trip. Why I was successful by not determining the 'how' was because the 'how' did not need to be predetermined. It *always* worked out when I let the "how" work out by itself. I began to understand that the universe is most adept at performing the 'how'. I could never match its powers. I did my planning and made the efforts that obviously belonged to me and then let the universe handle the undefeatable tasks. Each time, amazingly, it worked. I would watch when things just appeared to be occurring just right and people playing into the solution like it was scripted. I acknowledged to the universe that it was not this little ego that was responsible. That I believe is important.

The one time I deviated from this commitment to letting the universe handle the big issues, was when other people at home started to kibitz with advice on how I should do this work. Many suggested that I should bring my father home to the Midwest. I felt like I should listen to people since so many were saying the same thing. OK. I began following their advice and did the research, made the calls, setup the facility and went to Florida with a plan. Upon arrival at my father's placement, I prepared myself mentally to begin his transition back to the Midwest. Each staff person that I talked to, began to tell me how well my father was doing. One after another they said very positively, their pleasure of having him in the facility, without *any* prodding from me. It was amazing! I quickly retreated from all my preparation and realized what the message was that was being sent to me from all the energy bodies in my path. It was the right decision, retrospectively. Everything worked out better than I thought it would with a timing that only the universe could engender.

Whether, it is letting the universe do the complex 'how' or listening to the universe when we may be competing against ourselves, it is imperative that we know the difference of whose turn it is to do the work. If it's not our turn, the universe will tell us and 'us' better listen-up. It's always in our best interest. The other caution is to know that the results are really never ours. Only the efforts belong to us. The efforts are the dharma, the duty we must do for our station in life. The additional advantage on focusing on efforts instead of results is that we do not get burnout. The results belong to the universe and the universe will not get burned out. Now this is true for even very positive outcomes.

Positive outcomes are not something we should be happy about?! Our happiness should never be affected by anything if we are truly streaming the Being state. But yes, we are not perfect and we all like the 'nice' stuff. The key here is that focus is on efforts not attachment to anything in a serious way except the Way. If we are going to be consistent with the principles of being, we do not get to be stuck on the 'nice' stuff. That is *not* to say, that you cannot enjoy life or the accouterments that life brings. To deliberately not try to enjoy them is not the Way. Enjoying life and its ephemeral joys is fine. Attachment to the finite and fleeting beauties is not recommended. These two last statements are reconcilable. Let me illustrate. I wanted to purchase an expensive professional camera in order to indulge myself in one of my passions, photography. I will have more time in the very near future and wanted to follow my bliss. I received the camera after much waiting and thinking about it. My happiness did not change nor do I expect it to change as a result of getting this camera. It is a very desirable object. It is quite sophisticated. However, it is just a camera, a tool that has nothing to do with my connection to Self. I know that I could <u>never</u> satisfy the soul's code with <u>any</u> attachment to temporal things. But it's not like I don't enjoy the camera. It satisfies a need, but not an inner need. The plenum of fullness, the contentment of the Moment, and the ananda of Being is what satisfies. There is nothing you can add to it. There is nothing you can take away from it. Its completeness does not compel buying a camera or not buying a camera. Outcomes with success in the drama are immaterial to the core of Being.

Outcomes are a part of the drama and give meaning to the

actors. These are the props we need for a professional

performance. Actors generally do not take the props home

after their stage performance. Remember who you are at

all times.

6 – SOME USEFUL DEFINITIONS/ASSUMPTIONS. "IS EVERYTHING ALRIGHT RIGHT NOW?"

In Social Work there is a central concept in the practice of Social Work that is necessary to preclude failure and assure success. That concept is transference/countertransference. Transference is when the client comes in and has a predisposition to believing that you the therapist have stereotypical characteristics like: not really being concerned about clients; about it being about the money; about not wanting to help me; he just wants to get me out of the door; it's about pretending to like me; etcetera. All this occurs without meeting with the therapist and testing these conclusions for validity. The therapist has counter transference when seeing a client and making unwarranted claims of characteristics, usually negative, sometimes positive. A sex offender would be a good example of a client that would cause some reaction in the therapist. "This client is a pervert. I feel disgust towards sex offenders and this guy has been convicted." You get the point.

There are strategies to handle the transference and finding and neutralizing the countertransference. Therapists typically, but really everyone, needs to handle their transference and counter transference. Handling it means first becoming aware that you are vulnerable to it at all times. The antidote is to practice constant vigilance. Without constant vigilance it will leak in and destroy objectivity and effectiveness. There are clinical terms for this type of self-observation. In this discussion the optimum tool is Awareness. This is the Awareness that is abiding in the Being state of consciousness. Both transference and countertransference interestingly have the past impacting on the present. If we are really maintaining our Presence in the Moment (using constant integrated awareness) we automatically are handling any past leeching in our relationships. The Awareness is always on. That is its nature. That is who you are all the time. When it is off, You are off. And when You are off, You become by default, the little you (the manufactured ego that is mind-based). The Awareness switch is always on. Think C.I.A., that is, constant integrated awareness. But practice non-thinking awareness, effortlessly. Remember Awareness does neither need thought nor the tool called the mind. Again, there is a distinction between self-observation and Awareness that must be iterated. Self-observation is an activity we engage in when we are watching ourselves with our mind. It is mind-based and mind-contained. It is limited awareness. It is temporary in nature. It needs thought. This level of awareness has utility but is insufficient to properly see the mind due to its inherent limitations. We routinely access

this. Awareness is consciousness- based.

It is. It is who we are. It is in the Being state. IT is outside

the mind. It does not need thought. It can objectively,

without judgment, see thought, the mind, and the ego. It is

our permanent self. The distinction between the idea of

self-observation and Awareness can be illustrated thusly.

<u>We watch ourselves in the mind</u>. In Awareness, *we watch

ourselves watch ourselves.* The difference is the difference

between heaven and earth. Awareness is only available in

the validity of the Moment. Be the Moment and we will be

the Awareness.

A couple of examples of how <u>not</u> to use awareness and

counter transference in our daily life are exemplified below.

One of my managers wanted to inspire objectivity by

lauding the fact that she, 2 or more years ago was able to

discipline a friend who had not been successful in achieving a reasonable work task. This manager essentially figured that since she was successful then, that would always be the case in the future and that she would be objective and fair with everyone. This is not an uncommon delusion. The only way to master countertransference is through constant vigilance. Not episodic proof.

Another manager believed that when there was a conflict of interest when his fraternity brother was involved, all he had to do was to waive his hands, say no, and magically, the conflict of interest would disappear and be satisfactorily put to rest. This complete lack of introspection was acceptable for him because he was the judge and the jury. He had nothing inside him to challenge his erroneous assumptions. The bureaucracy he worked for had militantly rejected objectivity and fairness, relying instead on the judgment of 'company' men. This is probably a good example of a lack of self-observation. This manager's denial system and the organizational pattern have teamed up to promote the status quo. A preliminary step must always be taken all the time to challenge ourselves at any moment about anything we think we know. If we really know everything then we would not be here today. Stop the 'stuckness' of knowing too much. Always be open to others considerations and challenges to our way of thinking. Locking down on one way is a recipe for failure. There is so much diversity, in the unity of the diversity.

I heard a story on NPR about motivating a classroom of grade school children with interesting projects. These projects had a 'future' benefit, just like going to school will give a future benefit of increased wages, ability to raise a family, and a better quality of life. The children felt that there was not enough impetus for them in the currency of doing their assigned tasks right now, to keep them interested. They needed something that rang loudly to them in the moment. To successfully carry on in their project, the project had to adapt to the children's needs. This is not unusual for children or adults. We can go with 'some' future and do. But if we do not get our intrinsic needs met in situ, in the moment, we rob the best among us to go forward. The Moment has a definite role to play in the human condition. It is my contention that if we increase our percentage of time in this state of 'no mind, less mind' and 'not controlled by the mind' status; then we have leveraged the ability to be greater as a human being and leveraged the possibility of large-scale change in society. **Sathya Sai Baba said,** ""If there is righteousness in the heart, there will be beauty in the character. If there is beauty in the character, there will be harmony in the home. If there is harmony in the home, there will be order in the nations. When there is order in the nations, there will peace in the world."

It all starts with us. *Everything is alright right now,* when we course the consciousness from the Being state in every Moment and we allow the Awareness to Be. The Bliss, clarity, connection, and fullness are the reward (without being the reward) for Being in The Moment.

Having this Energy as a basis for everything we do shall

result in us being integrated human beings that are *not*

needy and only thinking about the future. With this quality

of energy, there will be a concern for what is going on in the

reality of life now. The Present will not be robbed by an

<u>over</u> concern for the future. And, then the global impact of

Beingness will have a more visceral meaning in all of our

lives.

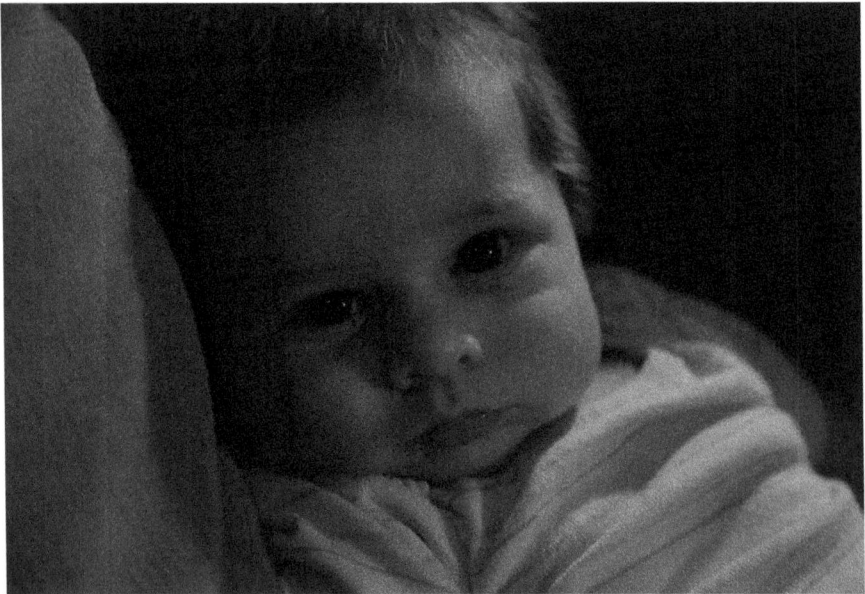

Mahatma Gandhi stated that we need to Be the change

we are looking for in our life. Being, like the pureness of a

neonate, is already there. Be that.

7 - PRESCRIPTION DRUG ABUSE, ALCOHOLISM, & CHEMICALLY ALTERED STATES OF CONSCIOUSNESS –Where am I right Now?

Societal sanctioning of 'legal' prescription remedies for specified 'medical' conditions has wrought an abuse that goes largely undetected or at least ignored by the greater population. The legality presumes an 'okayness' that has passed a threshold, albeit a legal one, and that is usually enough for most people to conclude indifference. This is not to say that this author is advocating illegal or legal drug use. But it is suggested that we are deluded more easily about any toxic side effects of abused substances, especially when they have a prescription or other type of sanctioning. This is not a time to be unconscious. In either legal or illegal use of substances, when there is a level of abuse/overuse, then there will certainly be a loss suffered to the evolution of the inner self. Why this deserves any mentioning in this particular context is due to the short-cut immediate delusion of achieving a desirable level of bliss through chemical means. That is, bliss that is chemically achieved, upon self. Dependence on substances has a deleterious effect on internal development. Recreational drugs are not the gateway to higher consciousness. They are not recommended.

In one's haste to rid oneself of suffering and exalt in the bliss of the Moment, we should not urge these ineffective shortcuts to become a strategy for change. The distortion,

confusion, and perseveration of egregious sensory input is

not the "middle way" the Buddha was talking about.

Certainly endorphin levels can be astronomically increased

to abnormal levels through ecstasy, crack,

methamphetamine

and

ayahuasca. Without an accompaniment of consciousness

that has a firm basis in reality, this temporary phenomenon

is precisely that, temporary. What needs to become

temporary and more liberated, are our patterns of behavior

to which we are locked down to in no uncertain terms. Our

freedom to get out of our 90% unconsciousness is

prohibitive without the elimination of these long-standing

patterns. Some of these patterns are not necessarily negative. Some are precariously negative. The 'negative' patterns of behaviors that consume us second after second, minute after minute, hour after hour, and so on, for the whole context of our life must be addressed in an overt way. These can be referred to as "vasanas" an ancient word that describes humankind's dilemma. To change one vasana in one lifetime is said to be a major achievement. How many people, relatives, friends, that we know, go from birth to death with no discernible hope of getting past these

obstacles?!

Getting drunk, imbibing psilocybin mushrooms, consuming inappropriate amounts of Vicadin will certainly change your view of things and give you a different perspective. However, the risks outweigh any short-term gain. The most powerful and underutilized method for getting past these entrenched vasanas, is Awareness.

Nothing can compare with the immediacy and safety of the

power of Awareness.

The Being state is always vulnerable to remission to

former patterns of behavior.   It is the Awareness piece that

keeps it from coming apart.   That is, C.I. A. (Constant

Integrated Awareness).   It is only through the <u>constancy</u> of

always being on, that it can really work.   Knowing the CIA

piece and knowing the temporariness of any alleged gain

through substance abuse, we know that they are not

compatible.   If you alter your consciousness with substances

you *immediately lose* your achieved Being state.   It is a loss

because it is a reduction in consciousness.   Your body,

brain, and systemic nervous systems are overriding your

ability to transact Self.   The stimuli are usually too great for

most of us to overcome. There is a story about Ram Das and his guru where the guru was given large doses of LSD with no apparent effect. This of course is anecdotal and the cited result is certainly unlikely for most of the world's population. As with an anesthetic, most of us would succumb to a loss of consciousness, enabling unfettered access to a surgeon.

In my adventures at the Burning Man art festival in Nevada, there were too many opportunities to indulge in the above activities of sensorial chemical delight. I was never really attracted to losing the natural high and immediacy of the Moment to a lesser vehicle. I felt connected to everyone through the Moment, as long as I was in the Moment. If I was not in the Moment, in the Satchitananda, I knew that the solution was not substances

but Awareness and my familiarity with how to get back in.
When you know the futility of going in a futile direction,
you know that the solution to your suffering is not *that*
quasi-traditional path. Instead of defaulting into a stupor
of questionable value, we need to question our patterns and
test out remedies that have a solid history of eff
effectiveness; to wit, the free and immediately available
methodology of Awareness.

Addiction on the other hand is a situation of excessive
abuse of self in sensorial, cognitive, and inner spheres of
being. There is no 'easy' solution for breaking the
establishment of pernicious habits. One thing that is clear is
that denial is not the path to liberation. Basil Braveheart,
an Indian medicine man and tribal leader who spoke on
Christa Tippits show on NPR, expressed his successful
approach to alcoholism. He spoke of how he, during the
Korean War, had engaged in horrific acts against the
population. As he was a human being, he engendered a

response probably similar to if not, PTSD. He indicated that he treated it with alcoholism. Only after he confronted alcoholism through his culture and after a dream (or vision) of contact with his ancestors, did it begin to abate. Sweat lodge time and other interventions had an impact. But what I found significant is what he said he does on a daily basis. Unlike a lot of Westerners who may put alcoholism in a closet, he did not. Instead he put alcoholism front and center in his daily life. It became his teacher. It informed him constantly. He, from this account did not mention relapse. In the town where he was previously arrested a dozen times, he became a significant leader.

There is no hiding and copping out as an adult. There is no place to hide. Denial may provide a respite or least give us an illusion. Denial of self is the result of refusing to see the trauma, the pain and the ugliness. Whether it's self-medicating for early traumatic events or addiction due to personal neediness, the solution has to start with seeing what is going on right now, in both external and internal views. Once real observation takes place, the problem is highlighted, acknowledged and there is movement from denial, pre contemplation, contemplation and then readiness for real change. Knowing how to have Awareness and where to procure it, is an essential starting point for the liberation of any addiction.

 Stages of Change: Pre Contemplation, Contemplation, Preparation, Action, Maintenance/Relapse.

8 –Energy out. "What am I exuding now?"

In Is it nonjudgmental? Is it full of love and compassion? Am I able to see myself in action without attachment? What am I exuding now, is a question that really comes from the Awareness piece, the piece that should always be present. However, one of the first clues we get we are slipping, is that the unabated judgment thing is happening more than once. This red flag is an indicator that the old pattern is kicking back in. And, we feel it in the Bliss department. When we are leaving the bliss of the Moment we experience a decline in our endorphin level that just doesn't cut it. Of course we should never 'force' feeling good. That is wrong at many levels, primarily because it becomes pushing energy. Energy likes to be led, not pushed. Energy by its fundamental nature cannot lie. So when we see a shift in the quality of our own energy, we see a correlate depreciation of consciousness in the direction of the mind, especially if judgments are being flung about. The strongest, best suited tool to correct this aberration is

Being- based awareness, the real you without the unnecessary structure of the ego. An effortless shift back to true awareness is possible if it is effortless and unattached. We cannot force it. Effortlessness is the natural state of this built-in aspect of consciousness. Effortlessness is the same degree of effort we make when we sign our signature versus when we try to sign someone else's signature. Struggle is superfluous and very ego-like. Iterating, you can't force bliss and you can't force effortlessness. These are in the being process, not the 'doing' we "normally" do everything with in life. There is a consistency, a uniformity of characteristics that are present but not bound in this Being/Awareness/Bliss. The mind is bound by time. The ego is attached and thrives in the unreality of past and future.

What energy we are is what energy we should be exuding. If we clearly see the quality of our energy we output, we can assess and troubleshoot. When the ego

93

comes into play, it is through attachment. Attachment is a struggle to control and dominate our own experience, things, and people. It is the source of suffering and is putting the false self in the way, resulting in compromised energy. By this definition, attachment disqualifies itself as a necessary ingredient of success on the path to getting ourselves out of the way. There is no need for attachment in the Being state due to this state of no-mind having a plenum of fullness that cannot be added to or taken away. When We are the basis for everything and everybody, taking on attachment would be ridiculously superfluous. The mind though, loves it. The mind mines attachment to survive and control us. The type and quality of energy we output is often compromised by ego, effort, attachment, working in the wrong time zone, pushing, and over-judgment. This is where to look when experiencing problems in the energy field.

Thinking errors are as common as thoughts. The

number one thinking error is thinking. We often overuse the tool and voila, over-thinking. *Over-thinking* is not the remedy to use when confronting a loss of vibrant energy. But that is what we first may opt for in a stressful situation. Our patterning designs it that way. When we don't need that particular tool and continue to use it, we hammer away with thoughts.

Do we really think we can solve our problem with compulsive thinking when that may be part of the problem? Yes we do. Have we ever thought that we should think less? Think about that! And then stop the unnecessary thinking. The mind is useful for rational thought and discrimination much like radar (a la Alan Watts). The radar needs to be shut down when the project/situation is completed. The problem is we never shut it down.

If we look at ourselves as being made up of tiny vectors of light with directionality in each arrow, it helps illustrate the point of how much energy are we dedicating to a certain

area.

As these arrows illustrate, our energy can be redirected (led

not pushed) in various directions, with variable intensity,

and with different qualities as this results in variable

outcomes. It is our energy and we load it up with our stuff all the time. We often do not have the vectors lined up together going in one direction (one-pointedness). More typical is the overwhelming distribution of vectors in the unrealities of the past and future with glancing moments in the eternal Present. So when we ask ourselves what we are exuding now, we should see the distribution of energy into how much unnecessary thinking and resistance to the Moment, how much Being versus reaction, how much intensity in the drama with reference to our Source connection, the degree of available Awareness, and finally, the quality of our effortless compassion/love we express outward. If we could visually imagine the honest directions our energies are taking, we can be more productive in maintaining 'Being', if that is what our goal really is in this moment. Energy does not pretend or lie. It can't. It's so beautiful because it's so malleable and honest. We can see more about ourselves (look at self-first) and others when using your energy to see and experience the energy of others.

By way of example, if you fell down in the proverbial street, a passerby saw you, picked you up, said nice words, and then left leaving you feeling 'bad' energy, after she had left, what can you conclude? It does not matter what you say so much, or what you do so much as the energy you honestly exude. We cannot hide our negative feelings even with acts of kindness or words of solace, if our energy is wrong. Conversely if our energy is right, our action so-so, and our word a little goofy, the thing that makes it right is the energy. Of course, if all 3 elements are correct then we have integrity and a virtual slam-dunk.

One of the other things that happen with our energy pattern is that we make an adjustment to instability as a reaction to instability. This adjustment would not be proper if our energy quality was stable and good. Just because someone is uncentered and angry does not mean that we need to make a change downward in quality to please the offending party. We should not find ourselves guilty just as a result of someone's negative state of mind. Our centeredness and good energy should not change, even with negative energy, if we are sourcing the Moment.

In a hypothetical room, there is an individual with energy that is being significant in its brilliance. Another individual comes in with low vibratory energy. It is incumbent upon the first person to not bring the brilliant energy down. There would be no reason to do it. Actually, there is good reason to continue the effulgent energy. Assuming that the energy was maintained in its brilliance, the being with the negative energy would summarily leave due to the 'un' comfortableness of this scenario. Too often we change our energy and accommodate the downward swing of quality and enable the negative energy to thrive. Stable energy needs to remain stable while unstable energy needs harmony. Maintain harmony with the universe through the Moment and create the milieu for optimal change.

In my experience in Criminal Justice, I had the obligation to visit a few judges in regards to some errors that were made in applying rules to interstate cases. My job was to repair the damage without offending the jurists who sometimes were reluctant to have their judgment challenged. In one case the judge allowed the convicted offender to leave the State without first securing permission from the receiving State. This offender had pointed a gun at a sheriff and at herself. This was not the case to send across State lines without proper documentation! My energy was good going in and good upon my departure from the judge's chamber. The judge however, was explosive and utilized inappropriate language when told that the order that was written could not stand. I believe the judge knew he was wrong and knew that the case had some dangerousness to it. He did holler a tad. There was no need to change the quality of my energy. It rocked without any arrogance. It was kind, direct, and cooperative. The judge knew what the right decision was and made it. I did not confuse the issue with any waffling. Happy trails, baby.

Another judge did have a legitimate problem with an officer's case that had some neglect. As I came in to see the judge, the sheriff said that my career could be over now, alluding to the strictness and 'take no prisoner' attitude of this jurist. I was not concerned. I was taking responsibility for the case and had no reason to change my energy. The judge is doing his job and is not any better than me (because he is me at the level of universality). Throughout the conversation with the judge I continued with the same good energy I started. The predicted gloom, shaming, raised cortisol levels, never materialized. As a matter of fact the judge appeared more content as we concluded. We handled the case. Good energy on both sides concluded the session.

9 –WHAT AM I DOING AND WHAT AM I BEING? KNOW THE DIFFERENCE.

Whatever we practice continuously will always show up in results. Practice or continued perseveration of a pattern will yield the appropriate result, all the time. Do we know what we are doing, thinking, acting most of the time? Most of our activities of living, to include times of not doing a specific designated task, will determine a pattern of behavior that belies our recognition by others, that is, a personality characteristic. Do we even see one-tenth of what we do during the course of a waking day? Do we have any idea of the percentage of time we think about a particular subject e.g. money, power, sex, God, boredom, pleasure, eating, feeling, escaping, loving, hating, or sleeping? What do we think about the most, most days- the non-thinking Moment? Most or all of it probably involves thinking, and thinking about things. How much time do we spend seeing the thinking? Can we spend enough time Being to see our thinking most of the time? How much time is dedicated to seeing through Awareness? If it's not 'constant' or at least a better percentage than when we pine our life overthinking things, we will NOT achieve the Being, Awareness, Bliss that is so fulfilling to our Soul's Code. To do less than half of our time in the Now, is to again make the choice to distribute our energy in a less productive and desperate way. To make the choice to Be in the Moment, constantly practicing effortlessly is to make the choice for the plenum of fullness and inner fulfillment, available only in this non-thinking consciousness.

Why practice? Why do something different? In life we all will suffer an avalanche of problems in a day that will upset our equilibrium and centeredness. Even if we understand some of the principles of how things work and the general rules of the Game, we will be no match for the fury of a difficult situation, unless the constant practice has occurred to endow one with the reintegration of the Self. When beginning this practice we will be no match for the aggression of some circumstances. It is only after a dedicated constancy of Being that this new energy will begin to be the energy of choice in circumstances stressful and 'un' stressful. We truly need to Be the energy.

Enlightenment does not come as a result of doing one technique or understanding one concept one time. It may seem instantaneous but that is only the appearance. If you look at the analogy of breaking a large stone, it does not break after twenty (20) blows with a sledge hammer. Another person steps up and after just one hit, the stone breaks. Was it the strength and technique of the 2nd person? Was it that the 1st person had done the preliminary work on the stone and the 2nd person had just concluded the activity? If we dig a hole in the ground looking for water, how do we go about it? Do we dig one hole for one hour and then go dig another hole for another hour, and so on? Or do we dig one hole and stay with the one hole for several hours? Assuming that there is water in both vicinities, it is of course wiser to pursue one-pointedness for a longer period of time. To split our efforts continually doesn't result in any depth or access to the deep-running waters of life.

Another factor is triggers. What is a trigger for one person is not for another. In Western modalities of psychotherapy it is well understood by competent practitioners that one technique cannot work well for all patients. Everyone is unique and requires adaptations and responses that are particular to the characteristics of each individual. If this wasn't the case then video treatment would be the more successful ticket.

In terms of what works here, it will be individual, as to what question, what narrative, what anecdote, what moment will uncover who you really are to you. No matter how the words are constructed here, it is always up to the reader to discover what works. Again, *these words* are just

the finger pointing to the moon. And if the trigger does

not happen after

reading words here or other words somewhere else, it may

mean that it is not time for what is needed at that particular

moment. You may be at a concert listening to some great

music and then It happens. Some irrelevant, seemingly

immaterial lyric breaks it all down to what it is. You have

gotten it, a total surprise and relief at the same time. Who

knows when or what or how?   When It happens, you just

know you know, at least for now. What a feeling! And you cannot explain it. If you try to explain it no one will understand, at least not what you got. So this is not a straight line or single method to getting there.

Once you get there, for even a moment, then the way should seem clearer. This is when the practices and new methods for Being become more important. Again, in my employment with county bureaucracy as a supervisor, I have had the pleasure to work with offenders who have had complaints, either about the system, their officer, or some knotty problem that they feel can only be solved through the intervention of a supervisor. This is good, I feel because the knottier the problem the greater the challenge and potential for satisfaction if resolved. The advantage in this situation is that the problems are easily articulated and because it is termed a problem then there is motivation on part of the offender to change. Without a problem, often there is significantly less likelihood of engagement in having a more immediate change in thinking on part of the offender (or ourselves).

One situation had to deal with a disparity in assessing two related offenders, sisters. One sister had been asked to come in at a rate of one-time per month and the other sister at a rate of two-times per month. Of course the sisters talked about the disparity between themselves. The one that was at my door overwhelmed her probation officer with her nonnegotiable anger. She was livid. Intuitively I grasped that the anger was not justifiable for this small matter. Instead of engaging on frequency, I focused on the anger. The issue revealed was the insensitivity of the bureaucracy. The case involved her sister being arrested and manhandled by the arresting officer; she intervened, jumping on the back of the policeman, resulting in her arrest as well as her sisters. The issue that prompted the initial arrest was questionable, the methods used were over the top, and the subsequent response was unacceptable, according to the 2nd sister. Then, going to report was only further insult upon insult. The fact that I immediately saw the issue facilitated the quick resolution of the initial anger and the trivial issue. Keys to success were no counter transference, no transference (from the offender) and a facile 'engagement' process. The ability to connect with as much pure honesty and authentic caring as possible, with no resistance (or fear) to the magnitude of the presenting problem, allowed a catharsis of the anger and movement/change to resolution. The moment, the awareness, and the Being state, the lack of resistance to the negatives, loving the uncertainty; are the factors that Social Workers do not normally talk about, but are factors that make problem-solving easier to do. The ongoing practice of getting out of the way all the time facilitates the engendering of an effortless and elegant solution.

The analogy of driving a vehicle needs to be revisited to further clarify a probable point we may ponder when facilitating the Present, that is, the future. Of course, it is

improper to live in the unreality of the future for all the

previously stated reasons. Moreover, it necessary to do

some planning in the Present for future events. If we want

to take a vacation in Lithuania, we need to get a passport,

airline tickets, hotel, and all the other miscellanea required

for the trip. Enjoying planning the trip is fine when

enjoying it in the present moment. Today, when I was

driving my vehicle, I was traveling at a high rate of speed

while turning down a two-lane ramp. Proper driving

technique requires looking ahead 25 to 50 feet or so, with

distance increasing depending on the rate of speed, all the

while being very present. When

traveling 50 miles per hour down a winding road we look

ahead and automatically we make the adjustments to our

driving motions in anticipation to what's forthcoming. If

we do not look ahead like this driving technique requires, we will have problems keeping up with the road changes and will have to make even more adjustments. This is analogous to how life works relative to planning. If we do not plan, we will not be effective in managing our travel through life. If we see the road ahead and make the adjustments in the Present without leaving the Present, we are most effective in handling any potholes that may appear all of a sudden. At the same time we can steer our vehicle to the right destination using proper technique and arrive safely due to proper mapping and forethought. Just like we have to be Present when we drive we must be Present when we live and plan. To do otherwise, is an accident of self, waiting to happen.

The Present and future can be manipulated by how we frame information.

Framing is a technique that we all should understand because it can be used in both constructive and debilitative ways. Politicians are infamous for using this technique to manipulate voters. Mother Theresa never went to an anti-war rally. She went to peace rallies. When we couch the concept in the negative, the negative is emphasized. "Stop the killing". This phrase has the operative word "killing". Not the concept you want to be sending messages about. "Love all, serve all." This phrase has tolerance, peace, and service wrapped up in four succinct words. Our words are powerful too, when backed up with integrity and authentic energy. We might as well get them right to serve us well. The subtleties' are important.

When we have a competing framework that is competitive to the Truth or is compromised by self-interest, prevarications, manipulations, etc., what we do not do is respond to the compromised framework. To respond to the compromised framework is to acknowledge the framework and give it instant validity. Not a good rejoinder. Rather it is wiser to respond with a different framing that captures the idea in a more appropriate,

friendlier way to what we believe is appropriate. And when

people respond to the new framework, then validity is given

to the idea and process. Society frames up a life of quiet

desperation as the norm. This low standard of existence is

accepted and unconsciously framed by the clear majority of

participants in this Western civilization. We define peace

as the period of time between two wars. Again, a low

standard is created. Our framing has the created the

critical mass of millions to engage in conspicuous

consumption at the expense of most of the world with little

to no care of consequences. We justify jobs as a carte

blanche to do anything to the environment. Our global

framing *ignores* the future ramifications of current actions

while at the same time ignoring the responsibility of duties

in the present. These are 'disconnects' with self and others

around us, the environment and economic prosperity, and

living responsibly in the Present without ego

aggrandizement. The framing is conveniently unconscious. Application of the Moment is an opportunity to leave the ego behind, move the false self out, and allow the universal, the Energy to come in the void. When you can be that, you can Be. And when you can Be, the universe will work through you.

The occasion came when an individual with an anxiety disorder (in my opinion) had asked to get some help after seeing a colleague. The ride on the El train had already added additional anxiety to the already anxious woman, who did not even want to get out of bed that day. Her mind was, according to her, out of control. She told of the time when she was slowly able to get out of bed and push through her day. Using an incremental strategy, of step-by-step, she was able to grudgingly get through her day, on some days. The strategy was difficult and borderline effective. It was not abating the issues. She was in my office this day. I accepted her pain and difficulty. We connect. The psycho-education of the Moment and reframing commenced. I ask her if she likes to be pushed. She states no. I ask what she does when the mind overwhelms her; she states basically that she pushes it away. And then the mind does what? She acknowledges the mind pushing back. I state that the mind is energy and energy does not like to be pushed. Energy likes to be led. We go through the basic principles of how things really work. We establish what the Being state is and how it is effortless. We establish the difference between self-observation and awareness. And we keep on connecting and loosening the bonds of attachment, especially attachment to the mind. Within 15 minutes there is a palpable difference from when she came in. She is no longer fearful; she is literally bathing in the energy of the Moment and the Being state. Her confidence has emerged and she is a new person, at least for these moments we exchanged energy. She was given written material to help keep her on her new experience of self and kudos for the fine work she did for herself in such a short time. As a postscript, her worker told me the next Tuesday that she had called his number on Sunday night and thanked him for giving her this opportunity to process this with me. She felt it worked.

My own take on the effectiveness of this anecdotal case is that we worked outside the traditional container of the mind. We left the mind behind for some new (but old) territory. This territory was not marked out by the mind nor ever could be. It was free of the traps and perseverations of mind-based weaknesses. Indigenous to this 'area' is the energy that comes with this space, that is, The Energy. As I told her then, The Energy can always do infinitely more than I can ever capture with words or actions. In this scenario, it is The Energy from my self talking to The Energy in her self. Be The Energy.

Be all you can Be.

DADDY'O

ABOUT THE AUTHOR

I am you in the deepest way. It is my pleasure to give this information so that I may benefit from The energy that is in all of us all the time. The details of my life are less important than the energy I exude consistently over time. This is my first book that is based on experiences in my 26 years at a local county office and 5 years of going to the Burning Man festival where I find the temple within and worship from there the whole trip. Aikido has also taught me about the quality of energy. Lastly, two pilgrimages to India have given me pause to ponder what is important in life.